PRAY MORE, LOVE MORE, SERVE MORE...
✦ Choose CHRIST ✦

MARCELLOUS FLOWERS

Contents

Contents..*v*

PRAY MORE...
1. SUBMIT TO GOD... 5
2. TRUST IN GOD.. 13
3. OBEDIENCE IN GOD... 23

LOVE MORE...
4. FAITH IN GOD... 35
5. DENY SELF... 41
6. SACRIFICE FOR CHRIST... 49

SERVE MORE...
7. HUMBLENESS OF CHRIST... 63
8. CONTENT IN GOD'S WILL... 69
9. GIVING GOD THE GLORY... 73
10. BONUS – FORGIVENESS IN CHRISTS' BLOOD............ 79

References..83
About the Author..85

PRAY MORE...

Luke 18:13- And the publican, standing afar off, would not lift up so much as his eyes unto heaven, but smote upon his breast, saying, GOD be merciful to me a sinner.

Romans 12:2- Do not conform to the patterns of this world, but be transformed by the renewing of your mind. Then you will be able to test and approve what GOD'S will is. HIS good, pleasing, and perfect will.

Romans 12:12- Be joyful in hope, patient in affliction, faithful in prayer.

"What are we going to do?" the kids asked. "We're going to pray and trust the GOD," I said, holding back tears.

It was a stressful time, but it was a situation I'd led them into before. Continued selfishness, pride, self-pity... just sin. **Proverbs 14:12- There is a way which seemeth right unto man, but the end thereof are the ways to death.** I justified my sin but was heavily in the Bible at this time. I was praying as well, but in this situation, in my eyes, there was no fruit.

There is always a point in your walk where you realize, it's not about you, at all. A moment when CHRIST becomes #1. Seeing how accurate Proverbs 14:12 is to us all. Even Christians tend to forget who it's about and I was getting a healthy dose of "who do you trust, yourself or ME?"

All these verses were popping up in my head-just a bombardment of biblical scriptures started connecting. It was like drinking water and realizing you were thirsty this whole time. Usually, in these types of situations, I'd hunker down and do, just about, whatever was needed to get out of it. That likely meant bending the scriptures to accommodate what was essentially not trusting The LORD. The world calls it being self-reliant. Most of the time, to Christians, it's putting GOD as our sidekick, and GOD doesn't like being an accessory in our life.

As we moved things into the apartment, I could see that their resolve was withering. All I saw in their eyes was, "Not again." I felt defeated. I felt deflated. I felt a failure, but there was a growing voice saying, "I AM with you here, now, and always." A quick prayer for strength to endure and find joy in HIM. I stood up in the fairly empty living room and said, "KIDS! living room." As they came with smiles that showed they were trying to keep it together for me. "Look, we are going to read the scriptures and pray every day and before we go to bed every night. EVERY NIGHT. If we want to blame, be angry with, throw a pity party, we will give it to The LORD and give thanks for all HE'S done for us. We're going to submit to The LORD and trust HIS will," I said.

They looked at me and had a different resolve. They were still gloomy, but a fire was becoming brighter. We locked hands, lowered our heads, and prayed.

1.
SUBMIT TO GOD...

Submission- The action or fact of accepting or yielding to a superior force or to the will or authority of another person.

Our submission to CHRIST is essential. Submission to CHRIST is a willingness. Submission to CHRIST is obeying HIS word. It's being CHRIST-like, and if our prayer life isn't consistent and submissive, how can we be CHRIST- like? If we live in rebellion to HIS commandments, how are we submitting to HIS will? If we believe it's ok to proclaim LORD, LORD, LORD, but not submit... we're double-minded.

We mask our double mindedness in an unstable way of living, usually some variation of self-help. One issue with self- help is... us. We set the parameters and move them as we see fit. What we see fit can very easily move to sin in seeking our own happiness or joy. The Bible tells us to seek GOD for our joy. To have our desires come from what HE'S set for us. The issue with having self-help is you're wrong from the start because CHRIST is usually not at the forefront of our being a better person.

We will look at examples of Biblical submission in the confines of marriage.

SUBMISSION TO CHRIST THRU MARRIAGE

How are we to be different from others if we continually speak GOD but don't live as CHRIST?

A recurring question that gets asked when discussing martial submission is, "Why should I submit when they aren't being CHRIST-like?" or "Why should I sacrifice when they aren't being CHRIST- like?"

ANSWER: Your submission to CHRIST, absolutely, has nothing to do with the other person. Let me say it louder for the people in the back.

YOUR SUBMISSION TO CHRIST, ABSOLUTELY, HAS NOTHING TO DO WITH THE OTHER PERSON!!!!

Each spouse has specific mandates CHRIST commands of us. When it's about what we want, how do we show CHRIST to the world, ourselves, or our spouse? That even, goes for us who have great marriages. If our marriage isn't built on the purpose of glorifying GOD, we're doing it wrong. This goes to all Christians. This is for those who believe in CHRIST and want to get closer to HIM.

We'll look at two examples of marriage, one shows abiding in CHRIST and one shows abiding in self.

ANANIAS AND SAPPHIRA

Ananias and Sapphira most likely had a marriage envied by a lot of people. They were there at the very beginning of the Church organizing. They came continually. They gave willingly. They loved the words Peter and the apostles were speaking. Yet, their hearts weren't really into this new teaching.

The issues that were tearing their marriage apart weren't between them. No divorce on the horizon. The two were in tune with each other. Their conflict was between them and GOD. Listen, no matter how AMAZING your marriage is, being separated from GOD is the path to destruction.

So, as they listened and adhered outwardly to the words and works of the apostles and the people around them. Who were finding their joy in The LORD, selling possessions to give to others with no intention of anything except glorifying GOD. They got caught in the whirlwind of giving but wouldn't die to self. That euphoric feeling when giving and others are giving, seeing the tremendous things being done. People thanking us. That's the problem, it's not for GOD.

Ananias and Sapphira went awhile in this bliss of surface-level faith. Eventually, they couldn't let go of the greed and pride within themselves. According to the scriptures, they sold a property of theirs to give all the proceeds to the Church. But, at some point, they both decided to hold some back and proclaim they gave all the monies. Who came up with the idea doesn't matter, they both were in on the lie. Essentially, they put themselves above CHRIST.

Marshall Segal, a staff writer for DesiringGod.org, wrote an excellent description of their great sin.

> "Because of their great sin, death did them part, that very day.
> Greed, that awful third strand in the cord of their marriage,

ruined them, derailed their souls, and left this couple for dead, literally, side by side in the grave."

The words Mr. Segal wrote resonates still today. Whatever that third strand of sin in the cord of your marriage is, it will destroy your soul. So, turn to CHRIST and put HIM first in your heart, mind, body, and soul.

As we continue, let's take a look at another example of marriage. One that, according to Book Three of the Stromaties of Clement of Alexandra, is an exceptional display of undying, unyielding, boundless love for The LORD and spouse. There isn't concrete evidence it happened but the crux of it is something we should strive for in our marriage.

THE APOSTLE PETER AND HIS WIFE

We all have an opinion on the apostle Peter. Most Christians identify with Peter more than anyone else in the scriptures. His inherent weakness and wishy-washy temperament are possibly most like all of us, who struggle with giving The LORD our heart, mind, body, and souls.

But, as CHRIST said what he would do, Peter changed, and that change was very clear and magnificent. He became a slave to CHRIST. The HOLY SPIRIT led him to otherworldly things. Peter didn't give the ole' "this is who I am" rhetoric. No, Peter submitted to GOD. He died to self.

When Peter was out of alignment in CHRIST, when the HOLY SPIRIT convicted him, he realigned with CHRIST, quickly. This story is a great antidote to display the undying servitude to CHRIST and the undying love to a spouse.

This story came to me through researching other references of JESUS, the apostles, and those that opposed and followed JESUS. Peter whom JESUS chose to start the Church. He stumbled in some very horrible and cowardly ways. He was called out by others. He walked away from CHRIST. He was like all of us.

The story goes, Peter was about to be, infamously, crucified upside down. His wife was to be murdered before him. As she was being taken to be killed, Peter didn't fight the guards, pray to be saved, or yell I love you to her. No, Peter did none of that. His words were so completely and utterly perfect; I got goosebumps the first time I read it. He sees his wife being taken to die, looks to her, and yells out, "Don't forget CHRIST!"

Now, if that doesn't make you want to give praise and honor to our FATHER. Peter's wife was so in love with GOD and her husband that she made the ultimate sacrifice. Peter cared about nothing else except she remembers CHRIST. Peter and his wife submitted even in the eyes of death. They took refuge in CHRIST. Will we?

2.
TRUST IN GOD...

Trust- Firm belief in the reliability, truth, ability, or strength of someone or something.

We have the inclination to insinuate that we trust The LORD in our lives. But, if we get to the heart of the matter, it would reveal how little trust we give GOD. It goes back to the beginning and continues today with Christians.

How do we get out of this self- destruction? How do we remove the fog of self-delusion? How do we begin to trust The LORD? In this section we will look at two examples of trusting The LORD: First, in the Book of Daniel with Shadrach, Meshach and Abednego. Second, through the Book of Job.

Shadrach, Meshach & Abed-Nego

As we step into the Book of Daniel, there is a theme of a few individuals who have complete trust in The LORD. What we also realize is that rulers, kings, and a lot of the people knew that GOD is the living GOD but their actions and attitudes, show that there was no real desire to place GOD first or at all in their lives.

We deceive ourselves into believing how we conduct ourselves selfishly is somehow for GOD. The "I wouldn't be feeling it so strongly if GOD didn't want this for me" attitude. How are we able to decipher what The LORD is thinking when we can't even explain our own behaviors.

King Nebuchadnezzar had an issue with putting GOD in HIS proper place. In the Book of Daniel, GOD has given HIS people to Nebuchadnezzar for worshipping many idols and being hard-hearted. He realized GOD as the GOD of gods, LORD of kings but still had little regard for GOD unless it benefited him. A level of distrust that is echoed today.

One of those times, He constructed an enormous golden image to worship. After calling all his officials to Babylon. The dedication turned into "a fall and worship this idol I built or be thrown into a fiery furnace".

Shadrach, Meshach, and Abed-Nego had an issue, right at their doorstep, at this moment. They could bow and not feel the wrath of Nebuchadnezzar or stand in faith to GOD. They displayed a trust that to this day is hard to come by. These young men stood not in defiance but trust. Trust in GOD'S word. The king hotly demanded they be brought forward. Furiously demanding an explanation for the disrespect towards his commands. These young men knew that if they submitted to what their king was commanding, it would show fear in him and not GOD.

We also need to remember; these were teenagers. These kids aligned themselves daily with GOD in the midst of losing their homeland and being subjugated to this new secular life. The resolve in GOD they must have had. Goodness. To keep the onus on GOD and have it not shift to them. That's a fine line to tow.

Walking up to the king, seeing his anger, frustration, and disbelief that these three captive Jews boldness. The audacity to challenge his authority. Seeing no fear in their eyes even as others looking upon this scene with sheer terror. But they had no worry but to make sure GOD was only praised. What a mighty GOD we serve.

The king gives them another opportunity to kneel to this idol. As the whole crowd watches Nebuchadnezzar fume with hate, threatening to throw them all into the furnace. The young men spoke, "O, Nebuchadnezzar, we have no need to answer you in the matter. If that is the case, our GOD, whom we serve is able to deliver us from the burning fiery furnace, and HE will deliver us from your hand, O king. **But if not, let it be known to you, O king, that we do not serve your** gods, nor will we worship the gold image which you have set up."

There's so much to unpack between the three gentlemen and the king.

1. They continued to show respect for the authority that GOD placed over them.
2. They made it clear that they wouldn't worship Nebuchadnezzars' golden image or his gods, whether GOD saved them or not.
3. They kept the conversation towards the king and didn't turn it into a sounding board that would take the onus off their trust and reliance on GOD.
4. THEY SHOWED ABSOLUTE TRUST IN GOD AND HIS WORD.

Obviously, Nebuchadnezzar didn't take the statements too well. He became so enraged with anger that he commanded the fiery furnace to be heated up seven times more. SEVEN TIMES MORE!!! Talk about angry, and never did the three young men waver in their trust in GOD. They knew whatever happened was GOD'S will, for GOD'S glory and to honor GOD.

Nebuchadnezzar watched as the men assigned to throw them in the furnace be incinerated. A certain satisfaction crosses his face knowing the lasting example of the wrath in store for those who defy him. As he looks in the furnace and is astonished at what is transpiring. Not only were Shadrach, Meshach, and Abed- Nego unharmed but there was a fourth member. And Nebuchadnezzar called it correctly, it was the SON OF GOD. This heretic, non-fearing, idol-worshipping, prideful man identified the SON OF GOD. What a mighty GOD we serve.

The king has the young men pulled out to give recognition to their GOD. He went so far as to set a decree that if anyone speaks amiss of the GOD of Shadrach, Meshach and Abed-Nego will be cut into pieces, and their house will be turned to ash. This maniacal king understood who was the true GOD. But, it didn't sway him to submit to GOD.

Nebuchadnezzar was what the New Testament would classify as double- minded. He is inconsistent and unsteady. He wouldn't submit. He wouldn't let go of his pride. In the same vein as King Saul.

Do we trust in The LORD? Is it one of those, "I kind of trust HIM?" If it is, we don't trust GOD. JESUS made it very clear in the New Testament, we are either in the Light, or we're in the Dark.

JOB

There's this prevailing idea that GOD blesses with worldly rewards those whom HE'S pleased with. That is so far from the truth. It shouldn't be mentioned but it's not true. Scriptures show us GOD speaking very clearly that HE does good to those who are and aren't saved. The grace HE gives is to all, whether we deserve it or not.

Some quick truths about the Book of Job.

1. Job is one of the first, if not the first, writings of GOD.
2. Job was not an Israelite.
3. Job thought completing a checklist would ensure his prosperity.

If one Old Testament book was needed to give a snapshot of GOD, Job would be it. It shows GOD as all-knowing... the beginning and end, Alpha and Omega.

I AM.

Job was blameless and an upright man, one who feared GOD and shunned evil. It was said, "There was none like him on the Earth." An example of how devoted Job was when his sons would have a feast in their houses. Job would send prayers and sanctify them and rise early in the morning and offer burnt offerings according to the number of people there. He did this regularly.

One day the sons of GOD came to present themselves to The LORD, and Satan tagged along. After GOD exalted Job, Satan attacked Job's character. Satan concluded the only reason Job is so faithful is because GOD hasn't only blessed him but extended the blessings to everything connected to him. Satan thought if GOD took HIS favor off Job, he'd curse GOD. God knowing Job's heart allowed Satan to wreak havoc on his life.

Satan starts the same tactics, he tries to dissuade us. He attacked the people and things around Job. Job lost all his possessions and children in back-to-back events. In all this turmoil Job continued trusting GOD.

As this didn't give the desired effect Satan was expecting, he went back to GOD and boasted if Job's health was cursed, Job would surely curse GOD. So, God allowed it. Satan struck Job with boils "from the soils of his feet to the crown of his head." But, even with all this pain and despair Job was going through, he continued to hold GOD in high esteem.

Next, Job was confronted by friends that assumed he had committed some offense to GOD or he wouldn't be in the situation. Pigeonholing GOD into our idea of HIM always makes us look foolish, and that is exactly what happened with Jobs' friends. If we're being honest, we've been that friend in some way. We've all pressed upon a friend some warped ideology of GOD. It's like the story in the Book of John, of the apostles, asking JESUS whose sin made the man born blind? And JESUS explained, none, his blindness was to display the work of GOD. Sometimes our struggles are there to show our trust in GOD.

Job's friends continue presuming they know why these horrible things have befallen him. But, Job stands firm that he'd done nothing to deserve this treatment. As it gets to the point of a stalemate between Job and his three friends, Elihu begins to speak out against both parties. Elihu, the youngest out of the group, patiently waited to respond. He was taken aback by Job justifying himself instead of GOD. He was disappointed with the three friends because they spoke as if they knew what GOD thought. Elihu was the only one that proclaimed GOD'S justice, goodness, and majesty.

Shortly after Elihu speaks, GOD reveals his omnipotence to Job. If there's one thing to know about GOD is HE lets it be known very clearly, HE'S not at the behest of anyone. Job realized that regardless of things happening around him, to trust GOD.

More than likely, we've all been in some sort of disaster. We've all at some point asked, "Why us, GOD?" We've wavered on our trust in the good GOD has done for us. Job's trials should give us comfort. Not comfort in the ending but in knowing GOD is in control. Trust that GOD is in control. That HE is for our good for HIS will.

3.
OBEDIENCE IN GOD...

Obedience- Compliance with an order, request or law or submission to anothers' authority.

As we round this section out there's a common theme present all the way to the end of this book. The hope is you'll figure it out. But, back to prayer, it's going to take the right intentions. It takes being completely dependent on GOD. To be led by the HOLY SPIRIT is essential.

Understanding the concept of believing in CHRIST is being led by the HOLY SPIRIT because it's that love that compels us to obey. We have to live by the spirit, not the flesh.

Obeying GODS' commandments is pivotal to our prayer life. If you're acquainted with the Scriptures, it gets real easy seeing what HE commands of us. You can convince yourself that you submitted. You can twist situations and say you trust GOD. It takes a whole different level of delusion to believe you are obedient when it, clearly, isn't the case. In the Books of 1st and 2nd Samuel, we'll see the delusion of obedience and true obedience to GOD and how it affects, not only themselves but their whole family lineage. It should give us pause because our disobedience does ripple through our families.

KING SAUL

1st Samuel is an excellent case study on doublemindedness. Saul wouldn't get past his self. He used GOD as an accessory. And GOD doesn't work being an accessory. Throughout Saul's forty-year reign as king, he never prayed to GOD with a contrite heart and broken spirit.

Through the first seven chapters of 1st Samuel, we see a people who were doing what they thought right within their own eyes, following the world. Being led by the world, Israel demanded Samuel give them a king. But, GOD wanted them to see that HE was all they needed. GOD wanted Israel to willingly be ruled by HIS commandments. Sadly, they didn't want that at all. They wouldn't obey GOD. They were a stiff-necked group. So, GOD gave them a king.

Saul was the first consequence of that decision for a king. He wasn't a cocky or self-absorbed individual, at first. As a matter of fact, he thought low of himself. Somewhere along the way, it was more important to be approved by men. He effectively convinced himself that he was honoring GOD by doing what he thought was right in his own eyes. We should look at this story and see how we, as Christians, can make our minds believe whatever we decide it to.

Saul was a choice and handsome man, who was taller than any of the other Israelites. So, visually he fit the bill from an outward only assessment. But, he came from the tribe of Benjamin as the son of Kish. His tribe was the smallest of Israel. His family was the least of the tribes of Benjamin. Yet, Saul was prideful, conjured up by fear of criticism and the love of approval of others. Writing about Saul could be a book by itself. It's such a tremendous look at a person who is lost but believes they're in GOD'S favor.

Saul had a lot of qualities to be obedient. He was from the smallest tribe which could've given him humility. His family was the least which could've supplied humbleness. He wasn't vain as far as I could tell before he became king. He could've received all the validation he needed from GOD if he would've just put GOD on the throne of his heart.

Unfortunately, Saul's life up until being king only accentuated his own prideful nature. He was hiding when he was pronounced king. And, this could be misconstrued as humbleness, but that was not the case. We see over the next forty years his unwillingness to trust and to obey GOD.

At Saul's coronation, Samuel delivered a steering message for Israel to follow The LORD with all their hearts or be swept away. But, Saul wasted no time in showing how little he regarded GOD.

1. During a fight with the Philistines, Israel was having a hard time. Saul was commanded to wait for Samuel to make a sacrifice. Saul fearing he would be defeated made the sacrifice. Samuel rebuked him for disobeying The LORD. Somehow, Saul saw no wrong in his disobedience.
2. The command was simple, clear, no room for misinterpretation. He was to leave no trace of the Amalekites. NOT A TRACE. Somehow after the battle was over, the king and the best of the animals of Amalek were spared. When confronted with this, Saul argued that he did do The LORD'S will. Even with the sound of the animals behind him, Saul was adamant he obeyed GOD.
3. David went from a close ally to an enemy. Saul went from being relieved by David to jealousy and hatred. Saul sought on many occasions to kill him, only to have David be in a position to kill him. Then change his mind when faced with David's humility. David knowing he was chosen by GOD never took matters into his own hands. Saul never wanting to obey was tormented by his inadequacies and iniquities.

Saul is the best display of instability. He is the epitome of double mindedness. He was chosen to abide in GOD but looked inward and wouldn't let GOD abide. We can't allow our moralistic or legalistic ways to masquerade as following CHRIST. As much as we like to muddy the waters of Scriptures. The Scriptures are very clear. We are to glorify HIS name in everything. We have to reconcile ourselves to submit, trust, and obey HIS Word. Accepting all that comes from it, good, bad, and indifferent.

KING DAVID

A man after GOD'S own heart. That's the best compliment you can receive from GOD. A man in the midst of a world reeking with pride, selfishness, deceit, depravity, debauchery, and the gambit of indwelling sin. This man stood firm in his obedience to GOD, but David was a failure.

David's story is a beautiful show of obedience through failure. David messed up countless times but always got back in alignment with GOD. He knew GOD would forgive a repent heart. He never doubted GOD'S forgiveness. He didn't question his trials. He just stayed close to GOD.

For being a man after GOD'S own heart, David was put through some extreme hardships. Isn't it odd that GOD favored David, but allowed insurmountable danger in his life? Yet, we never heard David questioning GOD about his difficulties. He accepted that whatever was in front of him GOD was in control.

When we first meet David, it's clear he trusts GOD. He's just been proclaimed the next king of Israel and what does he do? He goes back to work. He didn't jump to grab his destiny, nor did he hide from the fact he would be king. He knew GOD would work in HIS own time. A clear and direct contrast to Saul's conduct.

David was a mess like we all are. He lied to Ahimelech the priest to acquire bread and Goliath's sword. His actions ended with Saul having Ahimelech killed. When asked why he betrayed Saul, Ahimelech's answer spoke volumes about the character of David. Ahimelech said, "And who among all your servants is as faithful as David..." It was known from every corner the obedience of David.

There was the time David almost killed Nabal and all his male servants. GOD worked through Abigail to stop David from seeking vengeance with his own hands. We have to remember David was used to fighting. David and his crew were no slouches. They were about that business. David's manhood was being challenged but David recognizing

GOD'S will in Abigail shows he put GOD first.

How about the time David allied with the Philistines. He almost went into battle with Israel, but GOD interceded and removed him from the battle. How ugly that would have been if he'd fought. What would've happened if David wasn't removed from the equation?

Even being confronted with the affair with Bathsheba, he simply stated, "I have sinned against The LORD." The words of a man that knew GOD would immediately forgive him and Nathan confirmed David was forgiving. A man that stayed obedient and faithful.

Obedience is one of David's loudest cries to GOD. He sought to be in complete alignment in GOD. He failed countless times. He stumbled throughout his life. It wasn't an ideal existence for a man after GOD'S own heart. But he sought what GOD wanted continually. What a show of obedience that we should strive for as well.

LOVE MORE...

1st John 4:19- We love because HE first loved us.

1st Corinthians 13:13- And now these three remain; faith, hope and love. But the greatest of these is love.

1st Corinthians 16:14- Do everything in love.

Love is perfectly defined in the Bible. It's perfect because GOD is love. HE gives us example after example throughout the Bible and our lives of love. We strive to love perfectly. But, it only comes from the overflowing love from GOD.

"It's not your place." "You have no right to say anything." "Don't you trust them?" "Shouldn't you be able to say something?" "This is wrong." "Yeah, but you deserve this." The thoughts were invading my mind. To say I was struggling was an understatement. It was a full-on battle and I was losing. My ego, my pride was showing like a peacock trying to attract a mate. I'd convinced myself it was not about me. I wanted that perfect love. I sat confused, agitated, frustrated. I was reading the Bible, praying, fasting, being frustrated with an endless amount of "unmet needs" from a spouse, and GOD. Begging for wisdom and discernment and sure enough, HE supplied.

"I'm trying to convict you," I said. "That's not your place. That's GOD'S place." the response came. Mic drop. It was like a baseball bat upside the head. A truly clarifying moment if there ever were one. A moment of realization that the issue was me. That regardless of what is going on around me; it doesn't change what CHRIST expects from me.

The passage, "...remove the plank out your own eye, and then you will see clearly to remove the speck from your brother's eye." That passage isn't for us to be clear of sin because that's unrealistic. It's there for us to have our heart, mind, body, and soul in GOD'S sphere. Mine was not in that frame of mind. It came from a self- righteous man who began bending the Word to serve my purpose.

A sobering moment that once I repented, GOD'S love began filling me up and overflowing throughout my life. Were there issues, old habits? Definitely. It's a battle every day, but we don't have to fight it. CHRIST will fight it for us.

Love isn't about us; it's about CHRIST.

4.
FAITH IN GOD...

Faith- Complete trust or confidence in someone or something.

Can we honestly say our faith is how it's defined? Or is it a sliding scale like most of our morals? Is the faith we should have in CHRIST complete? Do we constantly use the "a work in progress" mantra? Can we be honest with ourselves or will we continue to lie to ourselves?

We are commanded to renew our minds daily. To righteously judge ourselves. Look into our hearts and see where we place CHRIST. Are we honest with how little or no faith we have in CHRIST?

So much of the faith structure we live by is built on sand. It's a whole bunch of filler with a sprinkle of CHRIST. It's our biases and prejudices with GOD wrapped around it. Its roots aren't deep. Then we wonder why our house falls at the slightest issue. Why our tree's not growing. We become so delusional, our problems are caused by someone or something else. And, if we do see that we are the cause; we can't get past ourselves to submit to GOD.

GOD knows we struggle. We're born sinners. The Bible vividly shows our lack of faith. We can't in our own will be faithful. We can only achieve that through CHRIST by the HOLY SPIRIT. There is nothing we can do. Nothing in us. NOTHING. We are shameful people. Deplorable. Even in our self-pity, we lose because we sulk in what we can't do rather than what GOD will do.

In the stories to come, we will look at Lot's wife and the healing of the servant of the Centurion. We will see how their faith showed their true character.

Lot's Wife

A pillar of salt. All for not taking heed of GOD'S Word. She looked back. She may have been curious. It could have been rebellion. The reason, it doesn't matter. She believed in GOD but had no faith in HIM.

There's not a lot known about Lot's wife. We don't even know her name. But, the little we do, there's a lot to take from her. Things to help us understand how serious our faith is to GOD.

Lot's wife was consumed by the world's pleasures and all its treasures. She was consumed by Sodom and Gomorrah. She was consumed by sin. Her seed of faith was chocked out by the thorns of a self- seeking life.

They lingered in their place as the angels urged them to leave hastily. The angels had to literally drag them out. And, as they get to safety all but one remembered and feared GOD'S words to not look back. In an act of pure defiance, she looked back and salt she became. The two young daughters and Lot had fear in GOD'S word. They knew GOD'S word was sure.

Lot's wife lacked true faith. Similar to the Exodus Israelites it was a "GOD keep giving and I'll keep taking" faith. They lived in full pride of self. Not dying to one's self.

A similar fate awaits us when living a life without faith. When faith is based on met expectations; it's not faith. So, being truly honest about our faith is paramount. When we lie to ourselves, we lie to the people in our lives. We're to renew our minds daily. To judge ourselves so as not to be judged. To live by faith and faith alone.

The Centurion

JESUS coming down the mountain had just given the most famous sermon in history. The Jewish leaders came upon HIM with an urgent message. A Roman Centurion asked to have his servant healed. Forget that it was unusual for Jewish leaders to entertain Gentile requests. But, it's even more unusual for Romans, especially Roman leaders, to ask Jewish people for help.

A centurion was in charge of a centuria, the smallest unit in a legion. In the Roman army, a full-strength legion made up of about 6,000 men. The centurion was in charge of at least eighty men. He was used to being the man in his world. A Roman man who had seen the treatment of Jewish people, especially, in Rome. A Roman man who had grown up in a pagan world. He was a man of war. A man who subjected the Jews to the Emperor's rule. This Roman showed understanding, of CHRIST, way beyond what the elders comprehended. Heck, way beyond what his own disciples understood. It amazed JESUS. Amazed HIM. So, much so JESUS let everyone know, "...Not even in Israel have I found such faith."

The Roman didn't even feel he was worthy to have HIM in his house. His faith was so immense it didn't even need JESUS to be there. People, that shows a man who comes humbly. It shows a man having faith. A faith that would still be there even if CHRIST did nothing. That Roman soldier's faith wasn't contingent on if CHRIST saved the servant. That soldier had faith that JESUS was GOD and his actions showed as such.

Do we know what authority we are set under? Is our faith based on what we ask for and receive? Can JESUS look at us and be amazed at our faith? Or is our belief as the demons and Satan? Is our belief without submission? Is it without obedience? Is it a selfish faith? Because it's either faith or it's not. The Bible is very clear we will bear fruit. The centurion showed fruit by his actions. What do our actions show?

5.
DENY SELF...

Deny Self- To decide not to have something you'd like, especially for moral or religious reasons.

Can we get an AMEN!!! There's no good way to bring this topic up without drawing some err from a large group of people. We live in a world of SELF. SELF HELP, SELF LOVE, SELF IMPROVEMENT, SELF, SELF, SELF... The most asinine thing is people act as if it's a new phenomenon. As if it's some new discovery, but it most certainly isn't new. What did Solomon say in Ecclesiastes 1:9, **"...And there is nothing new under the sun."** If you read the Scriptures, it's abundantly clear that this attitude has been around since the beginning.

The Bible shows a world, a people, and evil running roughshod through it with no real regard for denying self. It's always been a superficial, egotistical, morally bankrupt situation since Adam and Eve bit that apple.

To deny oneself takes dying to our wants and desires that are not GOD'S will. It's understanding that we bring nothing to the table but our sin. We have nothing GOD would need in any capacity. GOD'S not Zeus. HE doesn't lose power if we don't give HIM enough praise or credit. And, there may be some laughs but look at how we treat GOD. We move the importance of GOD in our lives depending on how much HE does for us. If HE isn't doing enough, we move HIM down. When life isn't what we expect we change the rules to accommodate whatever sin we're in the midst of or moving towards. Sometimes GOD'S infinite love for us is confused with believing HE needs us. HIM wanting us, to some, looks a lot like HE depends on us.

The Scriptures teach a straightforward message that Paul, Peter, and all the others spoke and wrote as one account. Because, there's only one account, and it's unchanging. Yet, somehow it's become this outdated book. It's torn apart and a false narrative is pulled from the heap to fit whatever we want to exploit that day. The lie never stays the same for some. It never stays the same when confronted. It changes with the sin we're in at that moment. It becomes a book of moralism. A book of legalism. A book of judgment. A book to use on others. We don't look inward. Not realizing how much of a wretched person we are. We don't see that we need CHRIST because we're the problem. We're the issue that needs to be fixed.

We've given up on CHRIST because we can't get past ourselves. That's why we're confused by what GOD is calling us to do. We make it about us. But, it's not about us. It's about HIM, All about HIM.

We've been led to believe that we should be self-reliant with just a side of JESUS. I'll say it again; GOD isn't our sidekick. HE'S not something we bring out when we need that extra boost. Using the Bible to discourage something or someone from confronting us about indwelling sin. To disregard someone because to us, they're not worthy to talk to us about this stuff. Using the Word to argue about how right we are. Using CHRIST purely for our own pride's sake is not what HE asks of us.

When we look at examples of denying oneself, it tends to go to JESUS. As HE is the ultimate example of what denying self looks like to us. In this section, we are going to look at something different. We will be looking at the Books of Hosea and Philemon. In these Scriptures, we will see two different approaches of denying oneself for the glory of GOD, to show honor to CHRIST and submission to being led by the HOLY SPIRIT.

Hosea & Gomer

So, we are back with a story that's been told through the lens of love. A story that displays the ridicule, pain and rebellion CHRIST endures for us. HIS long-suffering and patience for HIS elect.

Understand at this time Hosea, by law, could have stoned Gomer or mistreated her badly. What he did was not for himself but to obey GOD'S command. It must have been a horrible feeling; the jeers, the looks, the gossiping. A man in the land of idols. A people doing what was right in their own eyes.

The looks he must have received for marrying a harlot. Friends distancing themselves as to not be associated with them. Hosea may have thought she could change or even why me. His reputation in shambles all for following GOD'S word.

He's hearing things about the kids not being his. She's disappearing with no explanation or blatant lies. Friends, family, and strangers saying, they saw her in places she shouldn't be, with other men.

Showing love doesn't work. Being irate does nothing. A man standing exhausted, defeated, and heartbroken at the steps of his house, wondering. The only thing he can hold onto is it's for GOD'S glory. Somehow HE'LL work in this disaster of a situation.

She may have wanted to be faithful. Having someone see something in her more than her body. It seemed unreal and a man of GOD. The thoughts that may have crossed her mind, "A person that loves me. A man that will not judge my past. But, what if he is just like the others? What if he can't handle my past? What if a better woman comes along? What if I get bored? What if this isn't what I want later? I can't be a good mother? Why am I seeking other men's attention? I don't deserve this. I feel the walls closing in. I have to get out of here. They'll be better without me. I'll be better without them. I deserve to be happy. I'm just going to do what I want, follow my heart." Or it could have been the thrill was gone. Sound familiar?

Who would've expected GOD letting one of HIS faithful servants endure such a tumultuous ordeal for HIS glory? To not let Hosea do what he wanted? Why would Hosea have to stand rooted, while everyone around indulged in what they wanted with, seemingly, GOD doing nothing?

What is it that you're holding on to that CHRIST is asking you to trust HIM? What have you disregarded because it didn't make you happy or excited anymore? What excuse are you saying to justify your disobedience?

Hosea continued heartbroken finding joy in GOD'S promise. In the fact, he was enduring this for a reason. The kids asking, "Where's momma?" Friends and family saying, "I told you so." Having to keep speaking GOD'S Word to people. Trying to show the goodness of GOD while in the midst of this. Others telling him, "If this is what GOD'S all about, I'm good." Then one-day GOD tells him to go find his beloved and redeem her. For him to bring her back and love her.

Gomer's enjoying the trappings of her iniquities. She's free, not tied to anyone. She's in control of her body. She's desired. Maybe, she's having a conflict within. She doesn't feel she deserves to be happy. He was too good of a man. They're probably happier without her. She may not have felt she could let that past go. The sin just continuing to eat at her. A mind jumbled. A double-minded mind. A situation that becomes worse when somehow she becomes a slave to be sold.

Hosea's walking through those vile streets. Areas where a "good time" is always looked for. The agony felt asking if they'd seen his wife. Those same looks, sneers, and stares. But, Hosea kept seeking his Church. He stood firm, unshakable being led by the HOLY SPIRIT. Hosea had his house built on the ROCK. He turns a corner and there she is, on display as if she's cattle. Approaching he feels sick to his stomach. The mother of their children. The love of his life stands chained as others examine her as if she's a piece of meat, with no regard for him.

Hosea stands in front of the seller, "That's my wife." The man looks around as if Gomer doesn't exist. He looks at Hosea up and down confused and amused, "Who her?" with a loud laugh, "No, no, no... she's a whore. My property and I do as I wish with my property." Hosea's anger builds up, but he keeps denying self, "What's the cost?" The man scoffs and belts out a loud laugh, "What a fool. A damn fool to love a harlot." Hosea pays the price. The man grabs the money and laughs as he walks away.

Gomer stands there speechless, humiliated. She's stunned by what she's just seen. Not only did this man of GOD come to this despicable section of town but he just bought me. He came for me when I left him.

She's scared of what horrible things he'll say and do. How stunned she had to be hearing the words Hosea spoke. Letting the past stay where it was... in the past. He gives her undying love, unyielding forgiveness.

This story isn't the image we see when we think about abiding in CHRIST. We don't envision GOD wants us to go through excruciating trials and heartache. The Book of Hosea is a complete 180 from the idea we have of what CHRIST is to us. Denial of self is giving up what is not part of GOD'S will. It isn't denying in certain areas of our life but not in others. No, it's denying in all areas for GOD'S glory. And the HOLY SPIRIT will not lead us into sin. If we believe that we aren't being led by the SPIRIT; we're being led by our selfishness.

If our denying of self is contingent on GOD not making our lives too uncomfortable, it's not the whole Gospel we're hearing. The Bible is a clear view of GOD looking for us to find our joy in HIM, through good, bad, or ugly. HE doesn't change. He is the same yesterday, today, and tomorrow.

Philemon & Onesimus

The Book of Philemon tells a story of two different ways of denying self for GOD'S glory. It echoes there's no specific way to deny self. One a master, the other a runaway slave. Both being transformed in CHRIST. The two of them being asked to reconcile and further the KINGDOM OF GOD.

Philemon was, more than likely, a rich man. He was also an elder of the Church. His house was a place of fellowship. Paul was a friend to him. He was likely with Paul when he set up the Church in Colossae. So, we have a really good look of someone of importance in the furthering of the Gospel. He probably felt disheartened by Onesimus running away. What he was being asked to do was to make a slave an equal. Paul was appealing to what CHRIST had done for him. What CHRIST sacrificed for him. To deny that pride.

Onesimus, a runaway slave, wanders lost with no real destination, but GOD knew. He was led to Paul, where Onesimus found CHRIST. I bet when he received salvation, he didn't think it would lead him back to Philemon. He didn't think he'd be tested that way. To trust GOD had it all worked out. As the Scriptures say, "And we know that all things work together for good to those who love GOD, to those called according to HIS purpose." It had to be shocking to hear Paul ask him to deliver a letter to his old master. The sheer dread that must have crossed his face. He probably had high hopes of what his life would look like after being saved. The questions. The second-guessing. The frustration. He is going back with no assurances he won't be killed, sold, or mistreated. Think of having to handle being asked something like that. To go back to a situation with no assurances of your wants, well-being. All you have is your trust in GOD.

What Philemon must have thought when he saw Onesimus. How he responded before and after reading the letter. The pride he must have swallowed. The example showed to those who knew what had transpired between the two.

It takes a lot of letting go of self-preservation or selfish desires. But, we're all called every day to do what GOD has in store to make us holy, whether it's good, bad, or indifferent. We have to get past ourselves and get back to GOD. If we're going to say we believe in CHRIST, it comes with denying self.

6.
SACRIFICE FOR CHRIST...

Sacrifice- To give up in favor of a higher or more imperative object or duty

We ask what we're sacrificing and why. We ask why we can't decipher what to do. When we're nice, there's this uneasiness of our motives. What is that anxiety we feel in ourselves? It likely stems from it not being for GOD or our relationship with CHRIST is not in good shape.

Sacrificing for Christ isn't that difficult to comprehend. It's quite simple, yet not easy. It is not complicated until sin gets in there. It just requires that we stop doing for us. So simply STOP. The problem isn't we can't stop. The problem is we won't stop. I just heard Puff Daddy in my head. Anyway, there's a huge difference. HUGE. The world and our pride feeds us this lie wrapped in a piece of truth and calls it truth. We use the same methods on Scripture in a way that distorts GOD'S truth. We don't really want CHRIST to get all the attention. HE'S just a means to an end, and that's not sacrificing.

Where do we find the ultimate sacrifice? JESUS OF NAZARETH laying down HIS life for us. How do we sacrifice when it's for selfish intentions? How do we find what real sacrifice is? It comes from getting closer to CHRIST.

Sacrificing for someone or something with no tangible benefits is hard. In this section, we'll be taking a look at Mary, the mother of JESUS, and Ruth, the Moabite. We'll take a good look at their sacrifice by trusting GOD.

Mary

The reputation we get in our lives has so much of an impact on us, even if we don't care what is said about us. It doesn't matter what part of that spectrum we're on; we want to uphold that reputation that we've acquired. Ever met someone who has a bad rep and they relish in it. Some of them never change because they feel no one will believe the change. The "if I can't get credit for it; why do it" idea. They walk around poisoned by bitterness and bound by their iniquities.

Mary could've gone down that road. Instead, Mary lived her life with her head up following and trusting GOD, even with the gossip that was surely heard. Mary's story shows a young woman who could've been stoned, divorced, or shunned by her family. She was well aware of what could've happened. GOD put her in a situation that was difficult to bear and dangerous, to say the least. She accepted what the angel, Gabriel, told her and sacrificed her reputation to please GOD.

I'm sure she didn't want the same ridicule as other women faced with that mark on them. She had a family name to keep clean, but she was rooted for GOD'S cause.

Reading her brief story is inspiring, just the strength this young lady had to have. There was no way she knew what GOD was going to do. She had no clue GOD would speak to Joseph. No clue if she'd be able to carry the sneers, accusations, the looks that inevitably followed her. But she made a decision to trust GOD, reputation be damned. The words of the world held no weight.

We don't hear about all the rumors and stories about Mary but there were plenty. One, I read about has her being impregnated by some random stranger. This stranger just so happens to knock on her door and proclaims to be Joseph. He lays with her and then abruptly left her. She was so distraught she made up the story about the angel and the immaculate conception.

I do get other thoughts about having faith in CHRIST. I do. It's a hard pill to swallow. I hear it all the time. It sounds just as ridiculous as Santa. Completely understand what you're saying, and honestly, all I have to say is I live by faith and faith alone. We sacrifice for GOD because we have that Everlasting Water.

Can we go through our life with the looks, sneers, gossip, backstabbing, two- facedness? Can we rise above the reputation we cultivated to honor GOD? To show our love for CHRIST? Mary was literally standing in the face of death, and she stood fearless because of her trust in GOD.

What it must have been like after JESUS was born, heck up until her death. The salacious things said to her face. The taunts, possibly, from her own family. A tough cross to bear.

Have you held something away from CHRIST because you couldn't bear being seen in a different way? Has GOD told you to step away from something or someone so HE could deal with it, and you wouldn't? When was a time you showed your love for GOD with all your heart, mind, body, and soul? Between you and GOD ask yourself, when.

Mary stood firm in what was told to her. She had faith in whatever transpired will be for GOD. She lost her desire to establish and keep her reputation. She sacrificed all that she knew to do as The LORD commanded of her. All because she knew that whatever was asked, it was for her good and was going to show honor, glory, and obedience to The LORD. Let us step into that space of Biblical sacrifice. A sacrifice that has GOD saying he is pleased with us. A sacrifice that changes our lives.

Ruth

If there's a list of stories that shows sacrifice, The Book of Ruth is one that ranks extremely high on that list. She shows light of abiding loyalty and devotion not easily matched. The story is such a contrast to the selfish culture we live in today. This woman had no obligation to stay with Naomi. In fact, staying with Naomi she was, almost, certain to die as a beggar. Ruth could've returned to Moab. She could've found another husband and worshiped the gods of her land. We have to remember Ruth was not an Israelite. She grew up worshiping many gods but Ruth was having none of that. She trusted in the GOD of Naomi and followed her.

What a GOD we serve. How great Elimelech and Naomi's household must have been that Ruth would forsake herself for GOD? Yes, she went with Naomi, but it was GOD she followed. The desire that burned within her. Her devotion and loyalty was to GOD through Naomi and her family's show of faith. The sacrifices they must have shown daily for it to be ingrained in her mind and heart.

There was another daughter-in-law, Orpah, that was given the same chance but she went back to Moab. She went back to what she knew and what she considered safety. She couldn't get past herself to trust the GOD of Naomi.

Ruth steps into the unknown with a faith that's inspiring to emulate. Again, the likely scenario is they become beggars on the street. They had no family, were women, and Ruth wasn't an Israelite. To the outside, she was a foreigner. But, Ruth, through her devotion, loyalty, and sacrifice, indoctrinated herself into their way of life. She walked into that uncertainty with faith, hope, and strength.

As Naomi and Ruth get to Bethlehem, they find Boaz, a relative of Elimelech, had a field to glean. Gleaning was the act of following a harvest so that what is left can be used for the poor and widowed. The act of gleaning was established in Leviticus. So, we see Boaz following what The LORD commanded.

Ruth finds favor with Boaz. She listens to Naomi's direction and submits to the customs. As well as, Boaz being an upright man of GOD. They got married and had Obed who had Jesse who had King David. It all worked for GOD'S will and glory.

Look at what GOD had in store for Ruth. There was no way of knowing that she would be a part of bringing the Messiah to this world. She became an Israelite in her heart, through and through. She sacrificed comfort for GOD.

We must desire that depth of devotion and loyalty for CHRIST. There has to be a sacrifice with us. How else do we live for CHRIST? We can't walk around with the attitude that, "It's about me." We can't ever feel we've sufficiently done enough. IT'S NOT! We have to trust CHRIST through all situations. All our obstacles, hurts, and pains.

Naomi and Ruth were put in a horrible situation. A loss of their providers and protectors. GOD had laid out a plan that they knew only came from HIM, not their will but GOD opened the door. And, even Boaz followed GOD'S commandments with the real possibility of losing Ruth.

They could've schemed and exploited their way into something that benefited them selfishly. Ruth could've gone back to her homeland and found another husband. They could've manipulated Boaz as Tamar did to Judah. But, she stood on the principles GOD imparted on her heart through how Naomi and her family honored and worshiped GOD.

It can be daunting to walk on that narrow path. It most certainly puts us in hard circumstances sometimes. We lose the why sometimes and don't see the good HE'S doing for us. We lose sight of what is good because it's not good enough. It becomes not enough whatever GOD has for us. We believe it's not worth the sacrifice. We deserve better. We're owed more. We've done more than enough for GOD. Sacrificed way more than we ever wanted to. Questioning if HE exists if we don't get what we want.

We live in ourselves so much, we forget that we're to glorify HIS name. The thing is what's for our good is to depend on HIM all the more. Sacrificing ourselves for CHRIST is paramount for our spiritual health and growth. We can't get there any other way.

SERVE MORE...

1st Samuel 12:24- But be sure to fear The LORD and serve HIM faithfully with all your heart; consider what great things HE has done for you.

Mark 10;45- For even the SON OF MAN did not come to be served, but to serve, and to give HIS life a ransom for many.

1st Peter 4:10- Every believer has received grace gifts, so use them to serve one another as faithful stewards of the many-colored tapestry of GOD'S grace.

"Are you ok?" asked my foreman. "Yeah, my fault just lost track," I said. "Alright, we need you, so let me know if anything is going on," he said. With a head nod, he went on about his business. As I finished up paperwork preparing to go home, I couldn't help but feel helpless about this world of mine falling apart at the seams. As the low sound of Matt Chandler plays in the background, all I hear is, "It's not about you." Lowering my head thanking The LORD for the reminder, something swells up within me. The weight lifted, and joy rushing back in whispering, "All things work for HIS glory."

Walking into the house, thankful to be home. All is not well, but it is well within my soul. The LORD'S supplying all I need and then some. The air changes as I get closer. A struggle going on inside to see the negative. To make it about me. And the HOLY SPIRIT takes hold. There's an echo reverberating in my mind.

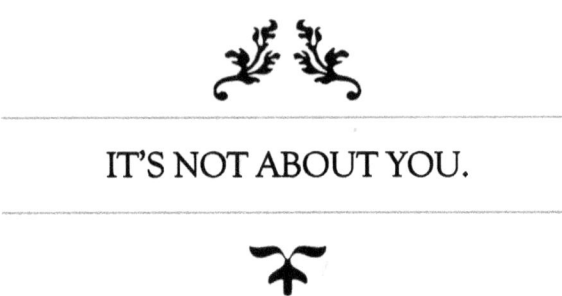

IT'S NOT ABOUT YOU.

Focused to just get lost in CHRIST. Let's run the laundry. Let's clean the room. Let's put the dishes up. Maybe vacuum the floors. Let's just do it for HIS glory. Thanking HIM for strength. Giving praise for HIS grace. In certain past situations, there would be an expectation. There would be self-gratification that had me above CHRIST.

Living in service to others is a touchy, steep, and dangerous trail to follow. One false step and it ends up being about you and what you've done. GOD'S laid out a roadmap that leads to fulfillment, but we have to be in alignment with HIM to read it right. Whatever map we're using that doesn't have the SPIRIT OF GOD leading us is the wrong map. And that map is leading us to darkness.

Our prayer life and abiding in GOD'S love will make serving others genuinely being about GOD. If it's not, trust and believe, we'll be confronted with our sin. We'll be admonished either by the SPIRIT or someone else, and it would be wise to listen to the message instead of who the messenger is. We quickly find ways to nullify the good news because the messenger is a sinner, but aren't we all?

Serving GOD is simple. It's not easy, not easy at all but it's simple.

The reason it's not easy is simple: **us**. Our sinful nature that wasn't taught but rather in our bones clashes with GOD'S Holiness. All those instances of kindness, being honest, holding my tongue, so many of them were, in essence, about me. I did it for a reason that had nothing to do with being led by anything but how it made me feel. Whether I wanted to feel better or worse, I did it for myself. Even when I conjured up a way to throw JESUS into it, it was about me. When we serve GOD it can't be for what we want unless we're in alignment with CHRIST.

The greatest example we have is CHRIST. This book could've dealt with all of the ways JESUS encapsulated every single topic. But, being able to see all these flawed people GOD used should inspire us to trust HIM all the more. So, in this section, we will look exclusively at JESUS. How everything He did was of service to GOD. In the remaining three sections we will look at CHRIST'S humbleness, humility, and glorifying HIS FATHER.

7.
HUMBLENESS OF CHRIST...

Humbleness- A quality of being modest or unpretentious.

He sits with the world in the palms of HIS hands. The judge of all that has come, that's here and will be. HE has complete control of everything that moves along the Earth. HE saw the vast emptiness filled in the beginning. HE should stand with an air of cockiness that is evident. But, all you see is humbleness. A humbleness that is only showing love and obedience to GOD'S will.

We are called to be Holy as GOD is Holy. Holiness is the name of the game. Our holiness has nothing to do with happiness. I would hear that phrase all the time as a youth. It never quite set in because I thought happiness and joy were one and the same. That isn't true. There is a stark difference between the two and it's not even close. Our joy comes from GOD and is an everlasting, unending water. Our happiness comes from our feelings that change depending on how the wind blows. What I'm saying is happiness is erratic, fleeting, continuously changing. It's the complete opposite of GOD'S joy. Being humble is a surefire way to live with joy.

Being humble doesn't mean thinking of ourselves as worthless or of little value. That isn't how CHRIST views HIS SELF, so how can we be CHRIST-like if we devalue who we are in CHRIST. Again, pride is the root of all evil. All our sin boils down to pride. Whereas, being humble leads to righteousness from GOD. Humbleness stands in direct contrast to what we, the world, and Satan wants from us.

CHRIST-like humbleness releases all selfish intent because we direct all desires toward GOD. You can't be prideful and humble at the same time. The two are at complete opposites on the spectrum.

In this section, we'll be looking at the story of JESUS and the Samaritan woman at the well. How JESUS crossed a barrier to reach someone for HIS FATHER.

The Samaritan Women at the Well...

It's hot in the middle of the day. JESUS needs rest. HE sends the disciples to get food as HE rests alongside a Samaritan woman. A woman getting water, oddly, alone at this time of the day. A woman we'll learn is in need of water, just not the water she's there to get.

Jews and Samaritans detested each other. Their hate was as such that even talking to each other could lead to being exiled from your community. The vitriol was high, yet here was the SON OF MAN offering this lady Everlasting Water.

This moment is a pivotal teaching moment, not only for the disciples but for us. The direct route to CHRIST is the best route to go, even if it's in, a perceived, enemy territory. It clearly shows CHRIST came to save all men. There is no bias with HIM, even if you have one. He carried no Earthly prejudices toward anyone. All of our cultural, racially motivated, financial, etc. biased thoughts and opinions are worthless endeavors to hold on to. One thing to realize in this story is GOD has no hang-ups about any of the petty things we hold on to so vigorously. When we boil it down, it's about our heart. Our submission. Our intentions.

HE approached this lady, whose life had been doing what she wanted to do. It had been her way since birth. You see, Samaritans had mangled the WORD OF GOD into a religion that acquiesced to their iniquities. Even though she had a faith in falsehood, just like any religion there's tremendous scorn when you go against their morbid principles. She was shunned in her community because of those sins. We don't know how she was known the way she was, but she had a reputation. A rep that stuck to her like weights she carried daily. She was pushed so far away, she wouldn't go with the other women in the early morning to get water. She feared the looks, whispers, or outright disgust from others. What are we holding onto? What do others believe that keeps you from seeking CHRIST?

JESUS saw the emptiness in her. HE saw the weight she was carrying. HE saw she was trying to be forgiving. HE saw all her sins in all their splendor, and humbled HIMSELF to lift her up. To carry that weight. To show she wasn't too far gone from GOD. That GOD doesn't care what she's done.

She was taken aback that this Jewish man was speaking to her. That HE was offering her water with no bucket. She yearned for the water that doesn't stop. An offer that most Jews consider was just for them. But JESUS was humble just to meet her needs. Needs that are offered to all of us.

She tried to dissuade HIM. She tried to start an argument about, the classic, "your faith vs. my faith." She wanted what JESUS was offering but wouldn't humble herself. She almost lost the gift. The way so many of us have been and are when confronted with the Living Water that CHRIST is offering freely. We risk losing it as well.

But, when JESUS finally breaks down her pride, she is overwhelmed with joy. So overwhelmed that she drops everything and heads to town to declare who had just saved her soul. This woman who feared everyone's words and looks went unashamed. Overjoyed to let everyone know who was at the well and HE'S coming for all who will believe.

The crazy thing about her going into the city proclaiming the MESSIAH has come and forgave her was people went out to see what all the commotion was about. They listened to a woman who wouldn't get water unless she was alone from the other villagers. She was a pariah, an outcast whom no one wanted to be around. Her testimony to this group, which already distorted GOD'S teaching, pegged their interest enough to go see JESUS, a Jew. Think about how awesome that is. Look at how The LORD can use the lowest parts of us to show HIS glory.

CHRIST demonstrated humility to this village that was culturally and religiously opposed to HIM. How the disciples must have felt seeing JESUS show humility to these people. He was humble enough to give GOD the glory. He was humble enough to save them from hell. HE'S trying to give us the same thing, so we can step out in this world and proclaim HIM like the Samaritan woman.

The act of being humble doesn't mean we're walked over. JESUS wasn't walked over. HE laid down who HE was to be emptied for our salvation. Let us pray to GOD for wisdom to understand what being humble is to HIM. Let's cling to it because we can't go to GOD being haughty and proud. So, let's empty ourselves for HIS glory because what's for HIS glory is for our good.

8.
CONTENT IN GOD'S WILL...

Contentment- Is the attitude of accepting whatever is provided for us, an being happy with it.

Being content isn't about settling for what we have, but having joy and trusting what GOD promises and has done. It floods over the greed, lust, and anxiety in our hearts. The disappointment that can cover us when GOD doesn't give us what we desire. It can move us out of being content. It can lead us to contempt. We move away from HIM and walk in greed, pride, and selfishness... a heart that gets harder as we continue down that wide-open path.

To serve others when we're not content with where we are in life is like swimming against a strong current. It usually doesn't end well. We have to get out of our own way and be content in GOD'S love.

Falling out of being content boils down to us forgetting who our LORD is and all that HE'S done. We don't lose our contentment when we know we have CHRIST. HE told Joshua, "I will never leave you, nor forsake you." That statement is just as reliable and dependable to us as it was to Israel. We have to stay content with CHRIST. HE has to be enough regardless of the outcome. In this section, we look at JESUS in the Garden of Gethsemane. We see that even in the face of death, CHRIST was content with what GOD prepared for HIM.

The Garden of Gethsemane...

After living the last few years homeless, JESUS approaches the end of HIS Earthly ministry. HE knows what lies ahead. HE'S going away from The FATHER for a short time. The presence that HE'S been experiencing since before time. The agony, distress... it was nearly unbearable.

HE took three disciples. Three to keep watch while HE went to GOD with grief so severe, HE sweat blood. HE cried for another way. HE cried to not be cut off from GOD for even a second. Yet, HE was content to do HIS FATHERS' will.

Understanding what's in store, HE submits to the will of GOD with the simple phrase, "Your will be done." That even to death, HE trusted GOD. Can we stand content in CHRIST even when we're told no?

We run. We hide. We act like the world and disregard GOD. We question GOD'S validity. We become delusional about what we expect. That we deserve whatever we desire. We have expectations because of our pride. We want because we make ourselves GOD.

When we live in contentment it's known who sits at the throne of our heart. We let go of that "me, me, me" mentality. We plead as JESUS did in that garden. We find comfort in what GOD'S done for and gives us.

Our intimacy with GOD loses its luster when we put things above GOD. When we desire the created instead of the creator, it's a disastrous situation. If we change our joy in GOD, we lose real joy. We replace it with happiness and that's fleeting. It's like a rollercoaster; up and down. Having joy in GOD is the most consistent feeling we can have. Please, don't lose it looking for something else.

Being content in GOD gives us strength so complete, our heart roars like a lion in the face of adversity. We see GOD fighting for us. HE comforts us.

JESUS was resolute to whatever GOD had in store for HIM. It

resonated to the Heavens all the way to the depths of hell. HIS secret was knowing nothing was better than GOD. The pure unadulterated gratification that spilled out to the world from HIS walk.

The life we lead in faith is so much better knowing that secret. The secret of being content, abiding, and obeying HIM. Confidence in the grace and mercy promised us.

Our life circumstances change, but GOD doesn't. Remember HE'S the same today, yesterday, and tomorrow.

9.
GIVING GOD THE GLORY...

Glory- To express admiration and praise for the excellency we see.

The idea is to love continually, giving glory to GOD in everything. How many can raise their hand because they do this every day? No one should have raised their hand. If you did, I pray that you would pray because we've all failed many times.

But there is "GOOD NEWS" for us. We have a savior, JESUS CHRIST, who died for us and sent down the HOLY SPIRIT to lead us to a personal relationship with GOD. The greatest relationship, I promise, we can ever have. The "GOOD NEWS" is such good news because it doesn't depend on us to be perfect. We depend on the SPIRIT to lead us to follow GOD'S Word. The Word that gives GOD all the glory.

The issue is we can't get past us. We're wired to make it about us; we relish in it. The world only enforces the "I" mentality with the bombardment of self-help, self- love, do what you want, YOLO, and all the other empty promises of fulfillment. The false promises that strain our lives to keep seeking it from other sources. All these sources being leaky cisterns and GOD has the only one that won't leak.

We become conceited, overly emotional, or desensitized because of the inconveniences in our lives. As well as us and how we are.

What if our thoughts got out to the world? We would shrink into oblivion with some of the stuff in our heads. We need a changing of the mind, that entails giving glory to GOD and getting off our high horse.

Coming to the end of this book, we look at JESUS. The time HE went to Capernaum and his disciples dwindled down to twelve. The SON OF MAN let go of men's adoration to glorify GOD. HE let go of the beginnings of an army, instead showing what is the priority.

WHO WILL ACCEPT IT...

"Most assuredly, I say to you, unless you eat the flesh of the SON OF MAN and drink HIS blood, you have no life in you." Pretty self-explanatory. Definitely direct. You have no hope, none whatsoever, without accepting CHRIST.

After hearing this, mummers went throughout the crowd. Many disciples were heard asking, "This is a hard teaching. Who will accept it?" When I was younger the thought was people didn't understand JESUS. They thought HE was talking about cannibalism, but I was so very wrong. Some definitely had that idea but most knew exactly what HE was saying. They knew but wouldn't follow. It asked too much of them, and that type of sacrifice wasn't part of the deal. They wanted the food, the security, the miracles but not to make CHRIST their everything. They walked away from eternal life. How far have we walked away? How many of us only want GOD for the miracles? Are we waiting, like Judas, for an opportunity to gain something using CHRIST? How many of us are benefiting off of CHRIST and glorifying ourselves? There's GOOD NEWS and that is every day you're on this Earth, you have an opportunity to turn for the first or millionth time back to CHRIST. DON'T WASTE THE OPPORTUNITY TO RECEIVE THE FREE GIFT OF SALVATION. TO GET BACK TO RUNNING THE RACE. It's here for you.

The great thing about this story is JESUS confronts these individuals with the truth to separate the chaff from the wheat. That's what the truth does. It makes us look at the real us. It cuts where we have to make a decisive decision on our faith. HE cut that group of thousands down to twelve real quick.

JESUS didn't let the crowd's words cloud HIS judgment. When the crowd tried to grab HIM and crown HIM king, HE left to talk with HIS FATHER. HE knew their reverence was false. He went and got strength. He got assured. HE got love that was genuine.

We have to be like Peter and the disciples. We have to stand firm in the truth, even when many walk away from it. Sometimes it's a loved one, sometimes it's peer pressure, sometimes it's our desires but when that truth comes stand tall on the rock of JESUS. As Peter said looking around as so many people were walking away, "LORD, to whom shall we go? YOU have the words of eternal life, and we have believed and have come to know that YOU are the HOLY ONE OF GOD."

> As we come to the end of this book, the hope is a more transparent and direct look at our individual actions, thoughts, and the real reasons for following CHRIST. Every section of "Pray More, Love More, Serve More..." can be interchanged. We can take out and put in different attributes of GOD. Humility, power, holiness, the list is vast. The only reasons these particular attributes made it in this book is prayer and petitioning for wisdom, clarity, discernment, and removing selfish ambitions. So, if you do feel lost, die to self and please, pray more, love more, and serve more.

Golden Nuggets of Wisdom...

"But the trouble is what we call asking GOD'S forgiveness very often consists of asking GOD to accept our excuse."
—*C.S. Lewis*

"The devil is a better theologian than any of us and is a devil still."
—*A.W. Tozer*

"You think this world owes you something. This world owes you nothing. Get over yourself."
—*Mom*

"I don't do this for approval of others. I do this for CHRIST."
—*Grandma*

"It's not about YOU!"
—*Pastor Matt Chandler*

"You know GOD loves you?"
—*Pastor Frank Wiley*

"We confess, but we don't forsake our sin."
—*Pastor Danny Gandara*

"Esau wasn't stupid. He just didn't care."
—*Pastor T.D. Jakes*

"What if our prayers were for others."
—*Pastor Darrell Stetler II*

"It's simple, but not easy."
—*Bob Goff*

"It's not your place to convict me. Only GOD can do that."
—*Stacy Catron*

"Why is the first commandment to love GOD with all your heart, mind, body, and soul?"
—*Deonta' Flowers*

"JESUS is always here."
—*Pastor Agim Shabaj*

"Is prayer your steering wheel or your spare tire?"
—*Corrie Ten Boom*

"As a follower of CHRIST, our greatest delight will always be found in our obedience to HIS Word."
—*Voddie Baucham*

"The cross shows us the seriousness of our sin- but it also shows us the immeasurable love of GOD."
—*Billy Graham*

10.

BONUS FORGIVENESS IN CHRISTS' BLOOD...

Forgiveness- The action or process of forgiving and being forgiven.

How can we forgive like CHRIST? The depth of selflessness we have to want the HOLY SPIRIT to take us to. No wonder it's one of the hardest things for us to do.

Our forgiveness lasts just long enough until the next issue crops up. Our forgiveness is like a cistern with cracks. We keep throwing fake forgiveness in it and it keeps leaking out. Then we keep repeating the same thing over and over again.

What about forgiving ourselves? How are we to forgive others when we can't reconcile with our faults, troubles, sin... our iniquities? We fail each other and CHRIST when we don't even allow GOD to show us what we are to HIM. When we stand and say we can't be forgiven. We won't forgive. How does that show what our LORD and SAVIOR have done for us? Show me someone who loves the LORD but thinks they can't be forgiven or forgiveness for others. It's double- mindedness. It shows GOD'S love, mercy, and grace aren't sufficient for us.

We forgive because HE'S forgiven us. As we go into this extra section, the focus will be on CHRIST on the cross. Enduring and persevering until the end for GOD'S glory. He ran the race set before HIM. HE sacrificed HIMSELF for you, for me, for us.

FORGIVENESS ON THE CROSS...

JESUS is the central figure of Christianity. HIS death was the culmination of a plan that had been set before time. The endless love of GOD spared us the destination that was so deserving for us. The degradation on the cross that HE accepted when there could have been legions of angels waiting to save HIM. But, with a heart set on forgiveness, CHRIST took all that was thrown at HIM.

There were chances for all to return to GOD. At every point, they had an opportunity to hear and see who JESUS was. The apostles scattered, mainly the women followed and watched as JESUS endured death. The slurs, hate, and beatings laid upon HIS body.

As HE'S dying, the well-being of HIS mother was important. Giving the thief on the cross with HIM salvation was important. While the guards are casting lots for HIS clothing and the crowds spewing hatred, HE asked GOD to forgive them. These spiteful, stiff-necked, hardhearted people with no ounce of care. He asked GOD to forgive them.

HE obeyed GOD unto death. HE stayed in GOD'S love. There's nothing more complete and fulfilling than being in GOD'S love. No wonder all the apostles and disciples sought to be in that love.

The Psalms give a great look into what being in and out of GOD'S love looks like. David pleaded with GOD to stay in that love. He yearns to get back to that love and that love pushes him to repent and change- desiring for HIS closeness.

CHRIST sat on that cross, knowing the agony experienced would pale in comparison to the glory GOD was to give HIM. He emptied HIMSELF to be the prototype to emulate in our walk in faith. Let us follow CHRIST for the sake of our souls. Let us be led by the SPIRIT that has the power to raise the dead, heal the sick, and lame. Makes the blind see, feeds the masses, rebukes demons and the devil. The SPIRIT that keeps our eyes on the things of Heaven.

REFERENCES

Tissot, J. (1886-1894). The Pharisee and the Publican (Le pharisien et le publicain). [Painting]. Brooklyn Museum, Brooklyn, NY, United States. https://www.brooklynmuseum.org/opencollection/objects/4532

Segal, M. (2020, May 12). For Better or Worse, DesiringGod. https://www.desiringgod.org/articles/for-better-or-worse

Burr, D. (2011). The Good Samaritan. [Painting]. https://www.danburr.com/religiousart

Farran, M.P. The Washing of the Feet. [Painting]. Conception, MO 64433, United States. https://www.printeryhouse.org/ProdPage.asp?prod=M10

ABOUT THE AUTHOR

Marcellous Flowers was born in 1982 in Oklahoma City, OK. Growing up, his grandmother had an immense shape on his faith. Being a single father, he continues that tradition. His hope is that this book leads you to get in a Bible. For you to pray with a heart for CHRIST. To let go of the things that are not of GOD. GOD bless you.

www.ingramcontent.com/pod-product-compliance
Lightning Source LLC
Chambersburg PA
CBHW070545030426
42337CB00016B/2360